Notebook for introverts

- This NOTEBOOK belongs to -

BRANDING BY Juls

www.ingramcontent.com/pod-product-compliance
Lightning Source LLC
Chambersburg PA
CBHW070643220526
45466CB00001B/273
9781691493487